Published by Kat's Socks

Bismarck, ND USA

Written by Kat Socks

Illustrated by Ben Brick

Edited by Annie Bennett

www.katssocks.com
www.picklesthedog.com

Printed and bound in China

Library of Congress Control Number: 2018943224

ISBN 978-1-7322448-1-8

PICKLES THE DOG

ADOPTED

Dedicated to all those who
have adopted animals.

Our animals are part of our family and I
can't imagine life without them. Every
animal deserves a loving home, and I
appreciate all the love and support that
animal shelters provide to pets in need.
This is why I give back in a special way, a
portion of Kat's Socks sales are donated
to animal shelters.

THANK YOU!

Thanks for helping
pets in a pickle!
Kat Socks

Welcome to our family!

I am your new sister, Kat,
and we live on a farm.

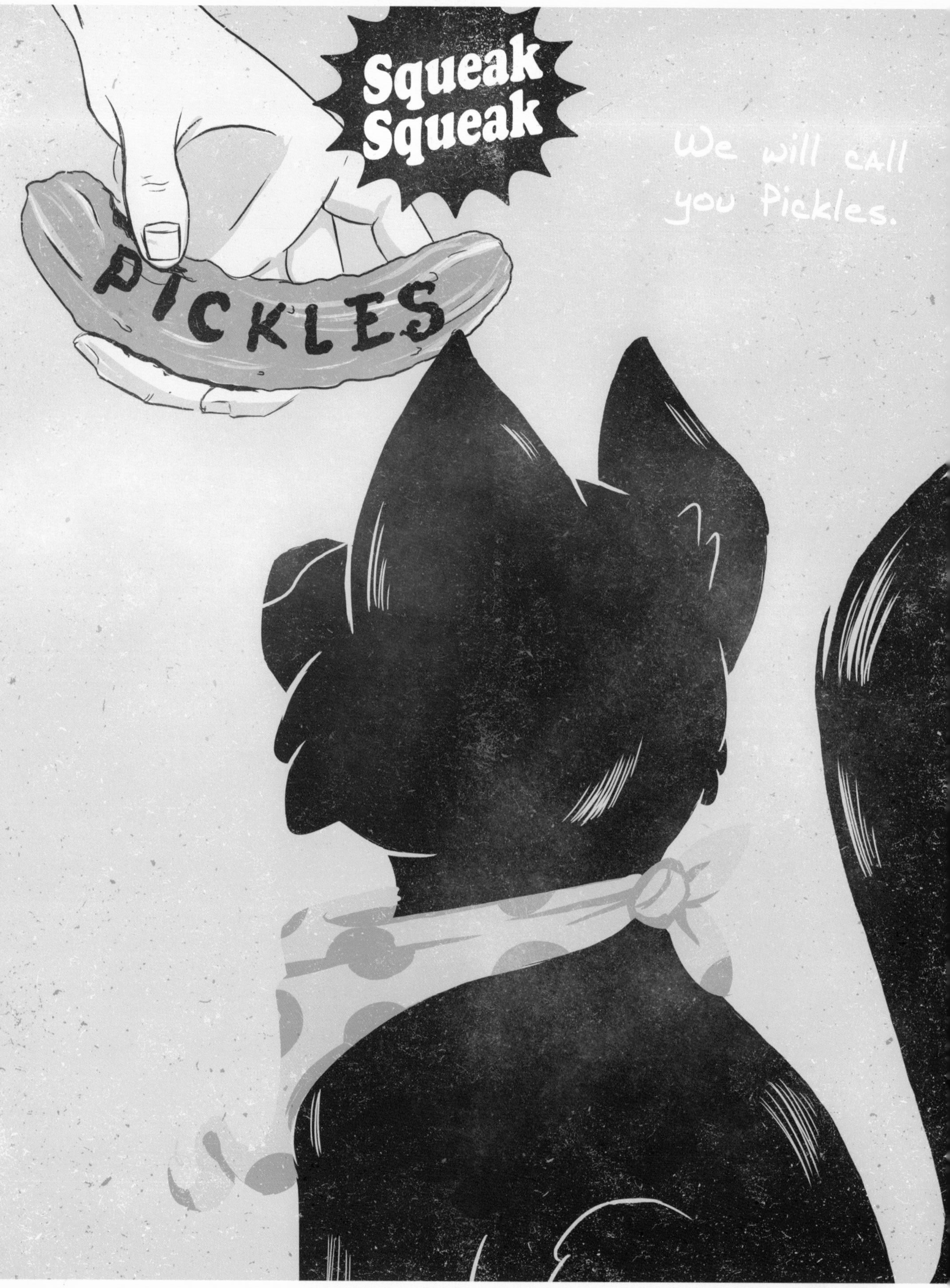
Squeak
Squeak
We will call you Pickles.
PICKLES

Hurry up, Ma!

Hurry up, Pa!

I want to get Pickles home to the farm.

Welcome to our farm, Pickles!

I can't wait to show you all the fun things we can do.

Oh no, Pickles,
you have mud everywhere!

Now you need a bath!

You look so nice and clean.

Let's go back outside
and meet the bull.

Pickles, no!

Don't pull on the rope!
Close the gate! Close the gate!

Oh boy, Pickles, you have a lot to learn.
That was a close one!

It's okay, it takes a little time to
adjust to a new home. Let's go meet
the cows.

Pickles, don't run!

Oh no! You knocked over all the milk containers! Let's clean this up. Then we can meet the chickens.

Good night.

First, we will check on the pigs.

Remember don't run in the mud, just stay next to me.

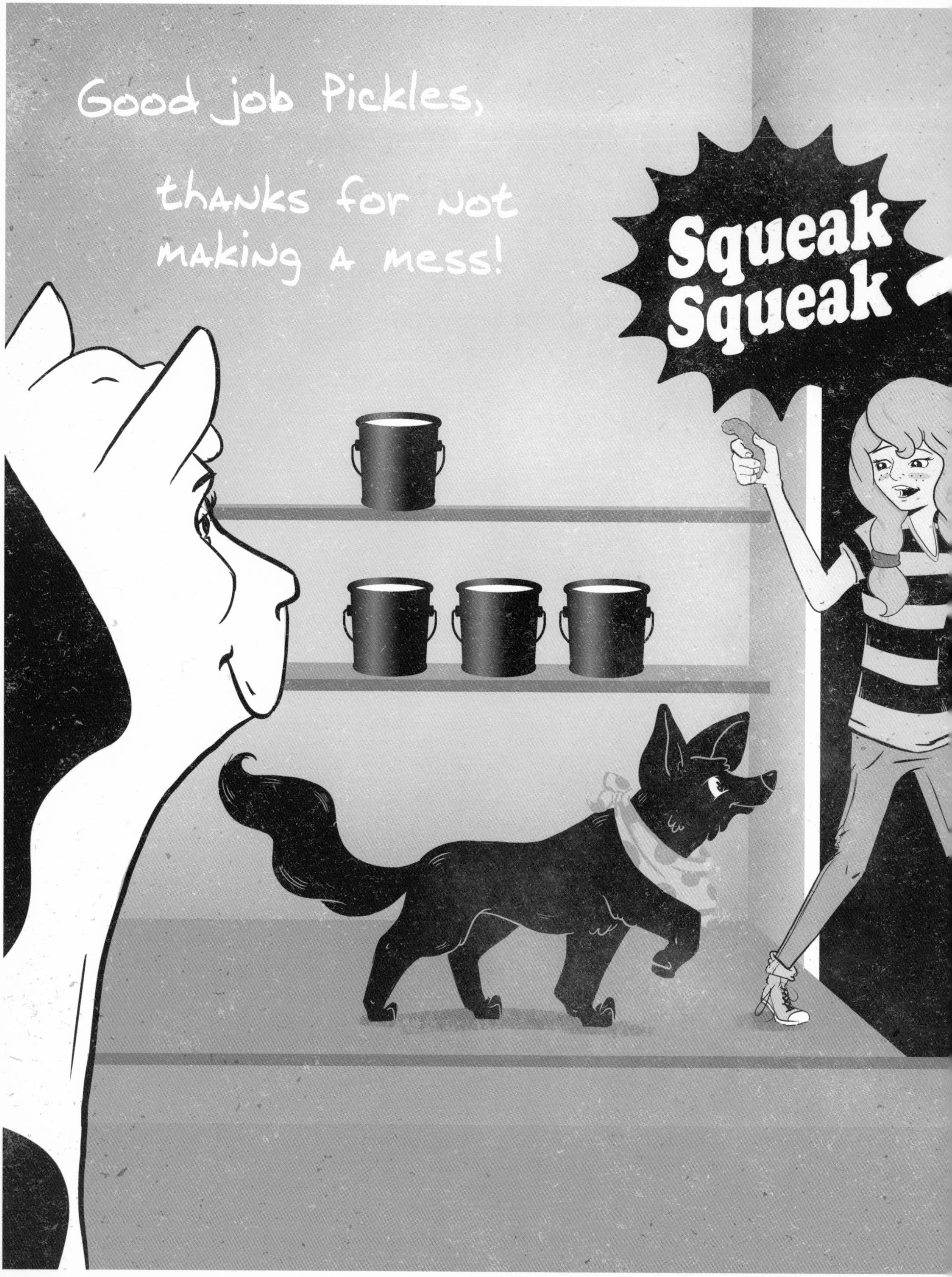

Good job Pickles,
thanks for not making a mess!
Squeak Squeak

You are a good girl,

you just needed a little
time to learn how to be
safe on our farm.

I love you, Pickles.